Trapped!

Written by Cynthia Rider,
based on the original characters
created by Roderick Hunt and Alex Brychta
Illustrated by Alex Brychta

OXFORD
UNIVERSITY PRESS

Please retu
the key
Keep dogs
on a lead

Gran took the children and
Floppy to see an old castle.

The children went up the path to
the castle. Suddenly, Chip stopped.

He pointed to a window at the top.
"Look, there's a face," he said.

Everyone looked, but the face
had gone.

"It can't be a face," said Gran.
"The castle is empty."

They went into the castle.
"It looks very old," said Biff.
"And very scary!" said Kipper.

"Let's play hide and seek," said
Chip.

The children ran in and out of
the rooms.

"I'll play too," said Gran, and
she went into the next room.

Gran looked for a place to hide.
She saw a gate and pulled it open.

CLANG! The gate banged shut.

Gran pushed it, but it was stuck.

"Help! Help!" she shouted.

The children ran to see what had happened.

"I'm trapped," said Gran.

The gate was very stiff.
The children pulled and pulled.
At last, it opened.

"I'll keep the gate open with this old chest," said Gran. "I don't want to be trapped again."

"Come on," said Kipper. "Let's see
where these stairs go."

They all went up the stairs.

Suddenly, they heard a noise.
Woo…ooo! WOO…OOO!
"What was that?" said Biff.

The noise came again.
Woo...ooo! WOO...OOO!
   Floppy pulled at his lead and
raced up the stairs.

"Come on! We must go after
Floppy," said Chip. They all ran to
the top of the stairs.

Floppy was scratching at a small
door. Gran slowly turned the
handle.

They saw a small dusty room.

"Come on, Floppy," said Biff.

"Let's have a look around."

Something went flapping across
the room.

"What's that?" said Biff.

Chip pointed. "It's an owl," he
whispered. "It must be the face I
saw at the window."

"Poor thing! It must have come down the chimney," said Gran. She picked it up very gently.

Gran took the owl over to the
window and opened it. The owl
blinked its big round eyes.

"Go on, owl," said
Kipper. "Fly away!"
The owl flapped
its wings and flew
up into the sky.

Kipper watched the owl fly away.
"It must be horrible to be trapped,"
he said.

"It is, Kipper," said Gran. "It is!"

Talk about the story

Rhyming pairs

Find the four pairs of things that rhyme.
Which is the odd pair out?

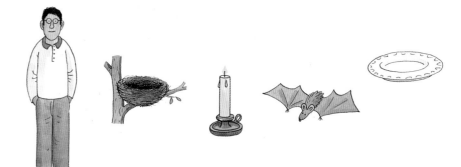